I0504153

DEDICATION

This Book is Dedicated

TO

My Family Members who supported me in all aspect

of life.

Especially to Sadaf Rasool

Computer Systems: A Comprehensive Guide to the Basics

ACKNOWLEDGEMENT

Writing a book is a collective effort, and want to offer my heartfelt appreciation to everyone who helped create "Computer Systems: A Comprehensive Guide to the Basics."

First and foremost, did want to thank my family for their unfailing encouragement and support during this journey. Your kindness and understanding have been a continual source of encouragement for me.

I want to thank the computer science professors and experts who have given their expertise and ideas. Your contributions have enhanced and expanded on the content.

I also want to thank the readers and students who will join me on this learning adventure. Your passion to study the world of computers motivated me.

Thank you for your support, wisdom, and encouragement to everyone who has had a role in this book, no matter how big or little. Your contributions have enabled this project to become a reality, for which I am eternally thankful.

Aaqib Nisar Bhat

bhataaqibnisar@gmail.com

First Edition

Welcome to "Computer Systems: A Comprehensive Guide to the Basics." In this book, we will explore the fundamental components, concepts, and principles that form the foundation of computer systems. Whether you're a curious beginner or someone seeking a refresher, this book will equip you with the essential knowledge needed to understand how computers work and interact with their environment. So, let's embark on an exciting journey through the world of computer systems.

CONTENTS

Unit 1: Introduction to Computer Systems

1.1 | What is a Computer System:

A Computer is a Collection of hardware and software components that cooperate to process and store data, conduct computations, and carry out activities. It is made up of a Central Processing Unit (CPU), which serves as the system's brain, and a variety of peripheral devices like as input and output devices. The operating system and the programs that allows users to interact with the computer and execute certain activities are included in the software. A computer system is intended to accept, process and send data in an organized and efficient manner.

1.2 | Brief history of Computer Systems:

The development of early calculating devices and mechanical inventions is traced back to the creation of computer systems. Here's a rundown:

1. Pre-20th Century:

- Abacus: A counting device used for arithmetic computations.
- Calculating Machines: Inventions like the Pascaline and Difference.
- Engine pioneered the use of mechanical equipment for calculating.

2. 20th Century:

- Vacuum Tubes and Early Computers: The introduction of vacuum tubes in the 1940s paved the way for the development of electronic computers such as the ENIAC and UNIVAC.
- Transistors and Mainframes: As vacuum tubes were replaced by transistors, computers became smaller, more dependable, and more inexpensive. Mainframe computers appeared, allowing huge organizations to have centralized computing systems.

- Microprocessors and Personal Computers: The invention of microprocessors in the 1970s enabled the development of low-cost, small computers, paving the way for the growth of personal computers (PCs) in the 1980s.
- Networking and the Internet: The proliferation of computer networks in the 1980s and 1990s culminated in the invention of the Internet, which revolutionized worldwide communication and information sharing.

3. 21st Century:

- Mobile Computing: The rise of smartphones and tablets resulted in   portable computers and broad on-the-go internet access.
- Cloud Computing: Cloud computing evolved as a notion that provides on-demand access to computer resources and storage over the internet.
- Internet of Things (IoT): The integration of computing systems with common things improved technology's potential, enabling for networked gadgets and intelligent automation.

Continuous developments in hardware, software, and communication have distinguished the history of computer systems, propelling progress and influencing the digital world we live in today.

Computer systems are classified into several categories, each of which is intended to fulfil a certain function. Here are some examples of popular types with simple definitions:

1. Desktop Computers:

- These are classic computers that are meant to be used on a desk or table.
- They include a separate monitor, keyboard, and mouse, as well as a computer tower housing the CPU, RAM, storage, and other components.
- Desktop computers are often powerful and adaptable, making them ideal for jobs that need a

lot of computing power, such as gaming, graphic design, and video editing.

2. Laptop Computers:

- Laptop computers combine the monitor, keyboard, trackpad, and other components into a single device.
- They are built for portability, allowing users to work, study, or surf the web from anyplace.
- Laptops include an integrated battery for on-the-go power and are suitable for those who want a blend of performance and mobility.

3. Servers:

- Servers are powerful computers that use a network to give services, resources, and data to other computers or clients.
- They are designed for great performance, dependability, and scalability, and are capable of managing many requests and servicing several customers at the same time.

- Servers are often used to host websites, execute programmes, store data, and allow communication in corporations, organizations, and data centers.

4. Embedded Systems:

- Embedded systems are specialized computer systems that operate within a larger device or system to accomplish specific activities.
- They are often found in daily products and equipment including as automobiles, washing machines, medical gadgets, and industrial gear.
- Embedded systems are frequently dedicated to a single purpose and have restricted user interfaces, functioning in the background silently to control and manage the device's activities.

5. Tablets and Mobile Devices:

- Tablets and mobile devices are small, touchscreen-based computers designed for mobility and interactivity by touch.

- Tablets, cellphones, and wearable gadgets are examples of such devices.
- These systems are generally used for communication, web browsing, multimedia consumption, and the operation of mobile apps.

1.4 | Key Components of a Computer System:

Each sort of computer system serves a distinct purpose, offering users varied degrees of mobility, performance, and functionality to meet their needs and preferences.

A computer system is made up of numerous important components that work together to complete different tasks. Here are the key components, with simple definitions:

1. Central Processing Unit (CPU):

- The CPU, sometimes known as the "brain" of the computer, is in charge of executing instructions and conducting computations.
- It interprets and executes instructions from the computer's memory, as well as performing

arithmetic and logical operations and coordinating the activity of other hardware components.

2. Memory (RAM):

- RAM is a type of temporary storage for data and instructions that the CPU needs to access fast.
- It stores data that the CPU is currently using, allowing for quick retrieval and processing.

3. Storage Devices:

- Hard disc drives (HDDs) and solid-state drives (SSDs) are storage devices that provide long-term storage for data, programmes, and operating systems.
- They save data even when the computer is shut off and provide long-term storage for files and applications.

4. Input Devices:

- Users can submit data and commands to the computer through input devices.
- Keyboards, mice, touchscreens, scanners, and microphones are examples of common input devices that allow users to interact with and operate computers.

5. Output Devices:

- Output devices display computer-processed information to the user in a human-readable format.
- Monitors, printers, speakers, and headphones are examples of devices that show text, pictures, sound, and other computer output.

6. Motherboard:

- The motherboard is a circuit board that links and holds the computer system's numerous components together.
- It offers the architecture for component connectivity and permits data and power transmission.

7. Power Supply:

- The power supply unit (PSU) transforms electrical electricity from an outlet into a form that the computer can understand.
- It provides electricity to all computer system components, assuring their correct operation.

8. Operating System:

- The operating system (OS) is a piece of software that controls the computer's resources and allows users to interact with the system.
- It handles memory and storage, supervises programme execution, and promotes communication between software and hardware components.

These critical components work together to allow the computer to analyse data, execute instructions, store information, and communicate with people, making it a flexible tool for a wide range of activities and applications.

Unit 2: Introduction to Computer Systems

Chapter 2.1|Understanding the CPU and its Role

The Central Processing Unit (CPU) is an important component of a computer system that executes instructions and performs computations. Here's a simple definition to help you understand the CPU and its function:

The CPU, sometimes known as the "brain" of a computer, is in charge of executing instructions and processing data within the computer system. It serves three key purposes:

1. Fetch: The CPU is responsible for retrieving instructions from the computer's memory. It retrieves the next instruction in the sequence and transfers it to the CPU for further processing.

2. Decode: After retrieving the instruction, the CPU decodes it to determine the operation that must be performed. It specifies the type of command as well as the precise data involved.

3. Execute: The decoded instruction instructs the CPU to do the actual operation or computation. It performs duties such as arithmetic computations, logical processes, data processing, and data transmission across computer system components.

2.2|CPU Architecture and Instruction Execution:

CPU architecture relates to the hardware design and organization of a Central Processing Unit (CPU). It covers the CPU's structure, functioning, and instruction set. Here's a simple explanation of CPU architecture and instruction execution:

CPU architecture describes how the CPU is internally constructed and how it interacts with other components in a computer system. It has registers, an arithmetic logic unit (ALU), a control unit, a memory management unit (MMU), cache, and buses. Data word size, instruction formats, addressing techniques, and available operations are all determined by the architecture. Each CPU architecture, such as x86, ARM, or MIPS, has its own design and instruction set.

The process of carrying out instructions stored in memory by the CPU is referred to as instruction execution. It consists of numerous steps:

1. Fetch: The CPU retrieves the next instruction from memory using the programme counter, which maintains track of the address of the current instruction.

2. Decode: The fetched instruction is decoded in order to determine the operation to be executed, the data involved, and the operand addresses.

3. Execute: The CPU executes the instruction's stated operation. It might include computations, data transfers, logical processes, or modifications to the control flow.

4. Memory Access (if applicable): The CPU may access memory to read or write data in some instructions. This stage entails retrieving data from memory or putting results in memory.

5. Write Back: Finally, the results of the executed instruction, if any, are stored back into registers or memory.

The instruction execution process is repeated for each instruction in a programme, allowing the CPU to do the appropriate computations and operations.

Clock speed, pipelining (overlapping instruction execution stages), and the existence of advanced features like as branch prediction and out-of-order execution all affect instruction execution efficiency and performance.

In summary, CPU architecture describes a CPU's physical design and instruction set, whereas instruction execution is the process of acquiring, decoding, executing, and storing the outputs of instructions within the CPU to accomplish specified tasks.

2.3|Introduction to Registers, ALU and Control Units:

Registers, Arithmetic and Logic Units (ALUs), and Control Units are critical components of a computer system's Central Processing Unit (CPU). Let's take a look at each of these components individually:

Registers:-

Registers are high-speed memory regions within the CPU that are compact and fast. During the execution of instructions, they store data, instructions, and intermediate outcomes. Registers are critical in allowing rapid access to commonly used data and enhancing the overall speed of the CPU. Among the most common types of registers are:

1. General-Purpose Registers: During arithmetic and logical processes, these registers contain data and interim results. They are used for a variety of functions, including variable storage and computation.

2. Instruction Pointer/Register: This register, also known as the Programme Counter (PC), maintains track of the memory location of the next instruction to be retrieved and executed.

3. Memory Address Register (MAR): This register stores the memory address of data or instructions that are being read or written to memory.

4. Memory Data Register (MDR): The data being transmitted between the CPU and memory is stored in the MDR.

Arithmetic and Logic Unit (ALU):-

The ALU is a component of the CPU that performs arithmetic computations and logical operations. It does addition, subtraction, multiplication, division, bitwise operations, and comparisons, among other things. The ALU acts on data stored in registers, executing control unit instructions. It performs the mathematical computations and logical judgements required for data processing.

Control Unit:-

The Control Unit is in charge of controlling and coordinating the actions of the CPU's other components. It interprets instructions, manages data flow, and directs instruction execution. The control unit reads instructions from memory, decodes them, and creates control signals to drive the ALU, registers, and other CPU components. It guarantees that instructions are performed in the proper order and that the necessary actions are made based on the instruction being processed.

Control flow choices, such as conditional branching and looping, are also handled by the control unit, allowing the CPU to change the program's execution path based on specific situations.

Registers, ALUs, and control units work together to execute instructions, make computations, and govern data flow inside the CPU. They are essential CPU components that allow it to do the necessary computations and operations in a computer system.

2.4 Overview of CPU performance and benchmarking:

CPU performance refers to how quickly and efficiently a Central Processing Unit (CPU) executes instructions and computations. It is an important aspect in determining a computer system's overall performance. Here's a quick rundown of CPU performance and benchmarking:

1. Clock Speed:

The clock speed of a CPU, measured in gigahertz (GHz), specifies how many cycles it can do per second. A faster clock speed leads in quicker processing. However, comparing clock speeds does not offer an accurate picture of CPU performance since differing architectures and designs might have an influence on efficiency.

2. Instruction Per Clock (IPC):

IPC, also known as Instructions Per Cycle or CPI (Cycles Per Instruction), is a measurement of how many instructions a CPU can execute in a single clock cycle. CPUs with greater IPC may complete more work per clock cycle, resulting in better performance.

3. Number of Cores:

Modern CPUs frequently feature several cores, allowing them to do various tasks at the same time. Each core may run instructions separately, improving the total processing capability of the CPU. However, because not all programmes can fully utilise multiple cores, the gain is dependent on workload and software optimisation.

4. Cache Size:

CPU caches, which include L1, L2, and L3 caches, are tiny, fast memory units used to store frequently requested data. Larger caches can boost speed by shortening memory access times and increasing data retrieval efficiency.

5. Benchmarking:

The technique of measuring and comparing the performance of CPUs or computer systems is known as benchmarking. Benchmarks are standardized tests that assess many elements of CPU performance, such as computational speed, memory access, and floating-point operations. SPEC CPU, Cinebench, and Geekbench are three popular CPU benchmarks. These benchmarks generate numerical scores that may be used to compare various CPUs or to measure performance gains over time.

It's crucial to remember that CPU performance is impacted by a variety of factors, including workload, programme optimization, memory speed, and overall system design. As a result, while benchmarks are a good starting point, real-world performance may vary depending on the use case.

When evaluating CPU performance, it is critical to consider the needs of your intended activities or applications. Because different workloads may prioritize different elements, such as single-threaded performance, multi-threaded performance, or floating-point calculations, it's critical to select a CPU that meets your individual requirements.

Unit 3: Memory and Storage Systems

3.1|Types of Computer Memory (RAM ,ROM and Cache):

In current computer systems, different types of computer memory are employed, each fulfilling a distinct purpose. The following are the several types of computer memory that are widely found in computers:

1. Random Access Memory (RAM):

- RAM is a sort of volatile memory that serves as a temporary storage location for data and instructions that the CPU need rapid access to.
- It is used to store programmes that are actively running, data that is being processed, and frequently accessible information.
- RAM is volatile, which means that its contents are lost if power is switched off or interrupted.
- RAM is important in determining system performance since it influences how quickly data can be read from or written to by the CPU.

2. Read-Only Memory (ROM):

- Non-volatile memory (ROM) stores permanent instructions or data that cannot be changed or erased.
- It is pre-programmed during production and keeps its content long when the power is switched off.
- ROM holds the necessary firmware, boot instructions, and system-level software to boot the computer.
- BIOS (Basic Input/output System) or firmware for embedded systems are examples of ROM.

3. Cache Memory:

- Cache memory is a tiny, high-speed memory that is situated near the CPU and is intended to boost system performance.
- It saves frequently requested instructions and data for quick access by the CPU, lowering the time required to get information from main memory.
- Cache memory is substantially quicker than RAM and aids in bridging the performance gap between the CPU and slower main memory.

- CPUs often have numerous cache levels, such as L1, L2, and L3, each with a varied capacity and access speed.

4. Flash Memory:

- Flash memory is a type of non-volatile memory that is widely utilized in devices such as USB drives, solid-state drives (SSDs), and memory cards.
- It can be electrically wiped and reprogrammed and preserves data even when power is disconnected.
- Flash memory is slower than RAM, but it has a higher storage density and is frequently utilized for long-term data storage in portable devices.

These numerous forms of computer memory collaborate to supply the storage required for various operations within a computer system. RAM is used for temporary storage of actively utilized data, ROM is used for crucial firmware and instructions, cache memory improves CPU speed, and flash memory is used for long-term data preservation.

3.2| Memory Hierarchy and the Principle of locality:

The memory hierarchy refers to how different layers of memory in a computer system are organized and arranged. The memory hierarchy is based on the concept of locality, which argues that programmes tend to use a small piece of the available data and instructions often and display memory access patterns. The memory hierarchy is meant to take use of this notion in order to improve performance. Here's how the memory hierarchy and the concept of locality work:

1. CPU Registers:

- Registers are the fastest and smallest storage units located directly within the CPU.
- They store little quantities of data and instructions that the CPU need rapid access to during instruction execution.
- Registers give the quickest access speeds because to their closeness to the CPU.

2. Cache Memory:

- Cache memory serves as a buffer between the CPU and main memory (RAM).
- It caches frequently used data and instructions in order to minimise the time required to retrieve them from slower main memory.
- The cache is divided into layers (L1, L2, L3), with each level increasing in size and latency while also offering more storage space.

3. Main Memory (RAM):

- The primary memory is main memory (RAM), which stores data and instructions required by the CPU during programme execution.
- It is greater than cache memory, but it takes longer to access.
- RAM maintains a program's active working set, which includes the presently executing instructions and the data they operate on.

4. Secondary Storage:

- Secondary storage devices provide nonvolatile, high-capacity storage, such as hard disc drives (HDDs) and solid-state drives (SSDs).

- They are slower than main memory but provide far more storage capacity for long-term data storage, such as the operating system, programmes, and user files.

To boost speed, the memory hierarchy makes use of the idea of locality. These are of two kinds:

1. Temporal Locality:

- The tendency of a programme to access the same data and instructions repeatedly over a short period of time is referred to as temporal localization.
- Cache memory utilizes temporal locality by caching frequently visited things so that they may be retrieved fast without having to continuously fetch them from slower memory levels.

2. Spatial Locality:

The tendency of a programme to access data or instructions that are near to one other in memory is referred to as spatial locality.

Cache memory takes use of geographical proximity by bringing in bigger blocks of data than are immediately needed, expecting that neighbouring data will be accessed in the near future.

Computer systems can use the principle of locality to optimize memory access times and overall system performance by utilizing a memory hierarchy that includes registers, cache memory, main memory, and secondary storage.

3.3|Secondary Storage Devices (HD,SSD,Optical Drivers):

Secondary storage devices are essential in computer systems because they provide long-term, non-volatile storage for data and programmes. They have bigger storage capabilities than primary memory and can store data even when the power is switched off. Here's an overview of three types of secondary storage devices:

1. Hard Disk Drives (HDDs):

HDDs are common mechanical storage devices found in computers.

They are made up of one or more rotating magnetic discs (platters) that are used to store data.

To access and alter data magnetically, a read/write head rotates over spinning platters.

HDDs are well-known for their relatively huge storage capacity and inexpensive storage costs per unit.

They are, however, slower to obtain data and feature mechanical components that make them more prone to failure.

2. Solid-State Drives (SSDs):

SSDs are a newer type of storage device that use flash memory technology.

They have no moving parts, making them more resistant to physical damage and faster in data access.

SSDs store data electronically on memory chips, providing faster read and write speeds compared to HDDs.

They are generally more expensive per unit of storage compared to HDDs but offer better performance and reliability.

SSDs are commonly used as the primary storage device in laptops, desktops, and servers to enhance overall system speed and responsiveness.

3. Optical Drives:

Optical drives use laser technology to read and write data on optical discs, such as CDs, DVDs, and Blu-ray discs.

These drives rely on the reflection and refraction of laser light to interpret the stored data.

Optical drives are primarily used for tasks like installing software, playing multimedia, or backing up data to optical discs.

However, their popularity has declined in recent years due to the rise of online content distribution and the availability of high-capacity flash storage.

Secondary storage devices enable the permanent storage of large amounts of data. HDDs provide cost-effective storage solutions with larger capacities, while SSDs provide faster access speeds and increased reliability. Optical drives provide a convenient method for reading and writing data on optical discs, but their use has declined as other storage technologies have advanced.

3.4|File System and Data Organization:

File systems organize and manage files and directories on storage devices such as hard disc drives and solid-state drives. They provide an organized method of storing and accessing data, allowing for more effective storage utilization and data administration. Here's a primer on file systems and data organization:

1. File:

- A file is a collection of data or information that is associated, such as a document, image, programme, or video.
- Files are usually organized hierarchically, with directories (also known as folders) holding files and subdirectories.

2. Directory:

- A directory is a storage location for files and subdirectories.
- Directories enable the organization and grouping of similar files, promoting logical organization and simplicity of navigation.

3. File System:

- A file system is a software component that organises, stores, and retrieves files and folders.

- It describes the structure and metadata associated with files, such as file name, size, creation date, and rights.

4. Data Blocks:

- Storage devices are divided into smaller components known as data blocks or clusters by file systems.
- A data block is the smallest accessible storage unit that generally comprises a set amount of bytes.
- Files are kept as a series of these data blocks, each of which contains a piece of the data in the file.

5. File Allocation Table (FAT) and Master File Table (MFT):

- A File Allocation Table is used by some file systems, such as FAT used in earlier Windows systems, to maintain track of the locations of data blocks assigned to files.
- A Master File Table (MFT) is used by modern file systems, such as NTFS (New Technology File

System) on Windows, to hold file metadata and file allocation information.

6. Hierarchical Structure:

- To organise files and directories, file systems employ a hierarchical structure, with the root directory at the top.
- Directories can hold files and subdirectories, allowing for logical data organization.
- The hierarchical structure facilitates directory navigation and contributes to a well-organized file system.

7. File System Operations:

File systems allow you to create, read, update, and delete files and directories.

These CRUD actions (Create, Read, Update, Delete) enable users and programmes to interact with the file system to manage data.

File systems supported by different operating systems include NTFS and FAT on Windows, HFS+ and APFS on macOS, and ext4 on Linux. Each file system has its own set of features, constraints, and performance characteristics that are tailored to certain use cases.

To summarize, file systems are systems that organise and handle files and directories on storage media. They offer an organized method to storing, accessing, and managing data, allowing for more effective storage utilization and data organization.

Unit 4: Input and Output Devices

4.1|Input Devices (Keyboard, Mouse, Touchscreens):

Input devices are necessary accessories that enable users to interact with a computer system by giving input or commands. Users can enter data, operate the system, and interact with apps through them. Here is a list of some typical input devices:

1. Keyboard:

- A keyboard is a major input device with a set of keys that represent letters, numbers, symbols, and function keys.
- Users use the keys to enter text, instructions, and other alphanumeric data.
- Additional keys for specialized functionality, such as multimedia controls or shortcut keys, may be found on keyboards.

2. Mouse:

- A mouse is a type of pointing device that generally has one or more buttons and a movable cursor control.
- To control the position of the pointer on the computer screen, users move the mouse on a flat surface.
- Users may pick, click, drag, and interact with graphical user interfaces (GUIs) and apps using mouse buttons.
- For added utility, some mice have capabilities like as scroll wheels or touch-sensitive surfaces.

3. Touchscreens:

- Touchscreen displays recognize and respond to touch motions, removing the need for a separate pointing device.
- Touching the screen with their fingers or a stylus allows users to engage with it directly.
- Touchscreens allow users to interact with apps and interfaces by tapping, swiping, pinching, and turning.

4. Scanners:

- Scanners are electronic devices that translate physical documents or pictures into digital representations.
- They scan printed papers and turn the content into digital files such as PDFs or picture files.
- Scanners employ optical sensors to convert a document or picture into a digital representation that may be saved, altered, or shared.

Other input devices include:

- Game Controllers: Joysticks, gamepads, and steering wheels are gaming-specific devices that allow players to control game characters or vehicles.
- Digital Cameras: Photographic or video capture devices that may be sent to a computer for storage or further processing.
- Microphones: Input devices for recording audio, allowing users to enter voice or audio signals into a computer system.

These input devices provide users a range of ways to connect with computer systems, catering to a variety of requirements and tastes. They make data entry, control, and interaction with programmes and interfaces more efficient.

4.2|Output Devices (Monitors, Printers, Speakers):

Output devices are computer peripherals that deliver information or results from a computer system to the user in a human-readable or perceptible manner. They display the computer's processed data, multimedia material, or answers. Here are some examples of typical output devices:

1. Monitors/Displays:

- Monitors or displays are the major visual information output devices.
- They display text, photos, movies, and computer-generated graphical user interfaces (GUIs).
- Monitors are classified into three types: LCD (Liquid Crystal Display), LED (Light-Emitting Diode), and OLED (Organic Light-Emitting Diode), with varying sizes, resolutions, and colour capabilities.

2. Printers:

- Printers are equipment that make paper copies of digital documents or images.
- They receive electronic files from computers and use inkjet, laser, or dot matrix technologies to convert the material to paper.
- Printers are often used for a variety of tasks, including the printing of papers, pictures, labels, and other tangible outputs.

3. Speakers:

- Sound or audio signals created by the computer system are produced via speakers or audio output devices.
- They let users to hear audio files, multimedia information, system alarms, or programme output.
- Stereo speakers, surround sound systems, and integrated speakers in laptops or monitors are all examples of speaker arrangements.

Other output devices include:

- Projectors: Computer-generated material is displayed on a bigger screen or projection surface using devices.
- Headphones/Headsets: Over-the-ear audio output devices provide a private listening experience.

- Braille Displays: For visually challenged users, output devices that translate text or graphical information into Braille characters.
- Haptic Feedback Devices: Tactile feedback or vibration devices that imitate touch sensations in particular applications or games.

These output devices enable people to observe and interact with computer-generated information or outcomes. They produce visual, aural, or tactile outputs, allowing for effective communication and use of computer-generated data or material.

4.3|Human-Computer interaction and user interfaces:

The research, design, and implementation of interfaces between humans and computer systems is referred to as human-computer interaction (HCI). It focuses on developing interactions that are effective, efficient, and user-friendly in order to increase user happiness and productivity. As the mechanism through which people engage with computer systems, user interfaces (UIs) are critical in HCI. Here is a primer on HCI and user interfaces:

1. HCI Principles:

Human-computer interaction (HCI) seeks to understand how people engage with technology and to develop interfaces that accommodate users' cognitive, perceptual, and physical capacities.

- It emphasizes user-centered design, in which users are involved throughout the design and development process to ensure that interfaces suit their requirements and preferences.
- Usability, learnability, efficiency, effectiveness, satisfaction, accessibility, and responsiveness are all HCI principles.

2. User Interface (UI):

- A user interface is the interface that allows users to interact with computer systems, software programmes, or electronic gadgets.
- User interfaces (UIs) include both physical (hardware) and software (software) components that allow for user interaction.

- User interfaces (UIs) give visual, aural, and tactile signals to users, allowing them to submit commands, modify data, and get feedback from the system.

3. Types of User Interfaces:

- Command-Line Interfaces (CLIs): Text-based interfaces that allow users to enter commands with precise syntax and keywords.
- Graphical User Interfaces (GUIs): Visual interfaces that assist interaction by using graphical components such as icons, menus, buttons, and windows.
- Web Interfaces: Web-based application interfaces that are available via web browsers.
- Touchscreen Interfaces: Touch motions and interactions are extensively employed in smartphones, tablets, and kiosks.
- Voice User Interfaces (VUIs): User interfaces that allow users to engage with systems through the use of voice commands or natural language processing.
- Augmented Reality (AR) and Virtual Reality (VR) Interfaces: Interfaces that enable users to interact with virtual objects or data in immersive settings.

4. Interaction Design:

- Interaction design is concerned with establishing user-computer interactions that are intuitive, efficient, and engaging.
- It entails creating the layout, structure, and flow of user interfaces while keeping navigation, information architecture, and visual aesthetics in mind.
- To promote successful communication between people and systems, interaction design also tackles feedback mechanisms, error management, and user help.

5. Usability Testing:

- Usability testing involves representative consumers in testing scenarios to assess the usability and effectiveness of user interfaces.
- It aids in the identification of usability issues, the gathering of user input, and the making of informed design decisions in order to improve the overall user experience.
- To measure user happiness, efficiency, and convenience of use, usability testing might include

tasks, questionnaires, interviews, and observation techniques.

Effective HCI and well-designed user interfaces are critical for providing users with intuitive and engaging experiences. HCI attempts to develop interfaces that improve efficiency, productivity, and user happiness across diverse devices and applications by understanding user needs, preferences, and capabilities.

4.4|Understanding Peripherals and their role:

Peripherals are external devices that connect to a computer system and provide additional functionality or input/output capabilities. They improve computer systems' usability, productivity, and adaptability. Here's a rundown of peripherals and their functions in a computer system:

1. Input Peripherals:

- Users can offer input to the computer system through input peripherals.
- Keyboards, mice, touchscreens, scanners, microphones, and cameras are examples of such gadgets.
- Users can utilize input peripherals to enter data, manage the system, capture photos or sound, and interact with programmes.

2. Output Peripherals:

- Output peripherals show or present to the user information created by the computer system.
- Monitors/displays, printers, speakers, projectors, and headphones are examples of such equipment.
- Users can utilize output peripherals to see visual material, print papers, listen to music, or present information to a wider group of people.

3. Storage Peripherals:

- Storage peripherals expand the computer system's storage capacity.
- Hard disc drives (HDDs), solid-state drives (SSDs), external hard drives, and USB flash drives are examples of such devices.

- Users can utilize storage peripherals to store and retrieve data, programmes, multimedia material, and backups.

4. Communication Peripherals:

- Communication peripherals allow computers to communicate with other devices or networks.
- Network interface cards (NICs), modems, routers, and Bluetooth adapters are examples of such devices.
- Communication peripherals offer wired or wireless communication, internet access, and device-to-device data transfer.

5. Multimedia Peripherals:

- Multimedia peripherals improve the computer system's multimedia capabilities.
- Sound cards, graphics tablets, MIDI controllers, and virtual reality (VR) headsets are examples of such devices.
- High-quality audio output, accurate graphics input, music composition, and immersive multimedia experiences are all made possible by multimedia peripherals.

6. Other Peripherals:

- Other peripherals include specialized devices like barcode scanners, joysticks, gaming controllers, biometric devices (fingerprint scanners, face recognition), and smart card readers.
- These peripherals are designed to meet the needs of certain applications, industries, or users.

Peripherals communicate with computers via a variety of interfaces, including USB (Universal Serial Bus), HDMI (High-Definition Multimedia Interface), Ethernet, Bluetooth, and Wi-Fi. They improve computer system functioning by letting users to interact with the system, save and retrieve data, interface with other devices, and enhance multimedia experiences. Choosing the correct peripherals is dependent on the users' unique demands, tasks, and preferences, as well as the computer system's requirements.

Unit 5: Operating Systems

An operating system (OS) is a software component that maintains computer hardware and offers a user interface for the computer system. It functions as a bridge between software applications and the underlying hardware, allowing for more efficient and regulated programme execution. Here's a primer on operating systems and their functions:

1. Hardware Abstraction:

- The operating system serves as a barrier between software programmes and hardware.
- It handles hardware resources such as the CPU, memory, storage, and input/output devices, shielding programmes from the complexity of hardware interaction.
- This abstraction enables software developers to create programmes that are unaffected by the hardware setup.

2. Process Management:

- The operating system supervises and controls processes, which are instances of programmes that are executing.
- It schedules processes, assigning CPU time and system resources to ensure that they run efficiently.
- The operating system supports the creation, termination, and communication of processes.

3. Memory Management:

- Memory allocation and management are handled by the operating system.
- It manages available memory and assigns memory space to processes.
- Memory management ensures that memory is used efficiently, including virtual memory approaches that make better use of limited physical memory.

4. File System Management:

- The operating system is responsible for file system management and offers an interface for generating, accessing, and organizing files.

- It handles file activities including reading, writing, deleting, and moving.
- Data integrity, security, and optimal storage utilization are all ensured by file system administration.

5. Device Management:

- The operating system oversees input and output devices like as keyboards, mouse, printers, and network interfaces.
- It offers a standard interface for apps to communicate with multiple devices.
- Device administration involves installing device drivers, performing input/output operations, and handling device interruptions.

6. User Interface:

- Users interact with the computer system via the operating system's user interface.
- Depending on the operating system, user interfaces might be command-line interfaces (CLI) or graphical user interfaces (GUI).

- Users can utilize the user interface to launch applications, access files, modify system settings, and do other operations.

7. Security and Protection:

- To safeguard the system and user data, the operating system applies security measures.
- To maintain data privacy and system integrity, it controls user authentication, access control, and file permissions.
- The operating system also safeguards the system from harmful software using built-in security methods such as antivirus software and firewalls.

8. Error Handling and Recovery:

- During programme execution, the operating system identifies and manages problems or exceptions.
- It includes systems for error reporting, management, and system recovery in order to reduce the impact of mistakes on system stability and data integrity.

- Automatic error recovery, system checkpoints, and system restoration options may be included in the operating system.

There are several operating systems available, including Windows, macOS, Linux, and mobile operating systems such as Android and iOS. Each operating system has unique features, capabilities, and target contexts, but they all fulfil the same basic function of managing computer resources and providing an interface for users and programmes to efficiently interact with the system.

5.2|Process Management and Multitasking:

Process management is a critical operating system function that includes the administration and control of processes, which are instances of running programmes. One of the most important features of process management is multitasking, which refers to an operating system's capacity to run numerous processes at the same time. An overview of process management and multitasking is provided below:

1. Process Creation:

- The operating system generates processes in response to user requests or the execution of system tasks.
- It gives each process a unique process identifier (PID), which allows the operating system to identify and manage it.

2. Process Scheduling:

- Process scheduling is the technique through which the operating system selects which processes receive CPU time in what order.
- The operating system uses scheduling algorithms to distribute CPU resources equally across tasks.
- Process priority, time-sharing, and resource availability are all aspects considered in scheduling choices.

3. Context Switching:

- Context flipping is the process of preserving one process's current state and restoring another process's preserved state.
- When a context switch happens, the operating system saves a running process's current execution

context, including its programme counter, registers, and memory state.

- The operating system then loads another process's preserved context, allowing it to resume execution from where it was previously paused.
- Context switching creates the illusion of numerous processes running at the same time.

4. Process Synchronization:

- Processes in a multitasking environment may need to synchronize their execution in order to share resources or coordinate their actions.
- To maintain correct coordination and prevent conflicts, the operating system includes synchronization techniques like as locks, semaphores, and monitors.
- When many processes use shared resources, synchronization methods assist to avoid data corruption, race situations, and deadlocks.

5. Inter-process Communication (IPC):

- Processes may need to communicate with one another and share data.
- The operating system includes IPC protocols to let processes communicate with one another.

- IPC methods like as shared memory, pipelines, message queues, and sockets enable efficient data sharing and process cooperation.

6. Process Termination:

- Processes may end when their duties are completed or due to incorrect situations.
- Process termination is handled by the operating system, which releases allotted resources and cleans up the related process data.
- The operating system or other processes can send termination signals to signify the need for a process to depart gracefully.

Process management enables multitasking, which allows many processes to execute concurrently on a single CPU or across multiple processors in a multi-core system. By creating the illusion of parallel execution, it increases system utilization, responsiveness, and user experience. The operating system's process management features assure effective allocation of CPU time, resource sharing, and process coordination, all of which contribute to the computer system's overall stability and performance.

5.3|File Systems and Storage Management:

File systems and storage management are operating system components that handle the organization, storage, and retrieval of data on storage devices. They offer a systematic method of storing and accessing files, guaranteeing effective data management and protection. An overview of file systems and storage management is provided below:

1. File Systems:

- The operating system uses a file system to store, organize, and retrieve files on storage media.
- The format, naming standards, and access mechanisms for files and directories are defined by file systems.
- They handle file metadata, such as permissions, creation dates, file size, and ownership.

2. Storage Devices:

- Hard disc drives (HDDs), solid-state drives (SSDs), and optical drives serve as the physical medium for storing data.

- The operating system communicates with storage devices via device drivers and controllers to read and write data to them.

3. Disk Partitioning:

- Disc partitioning is the process of dividing a physical storage device into many logical pieces known as partitions.
- Each partition can be formatted with a file system and appears to the operating system as a distinct storage unit.
- Partitioning allows the system to manage several file systems while also providing data segregation and organization.

4. File Allocation Methods:

- How files are stored and accessed on a storage device is determined by file allocation mechanisms.
- Contiguous allocation, linked allocation, indexed allocation, and a mix of these approaches are common file allocation strategies.
- The allocation mechanism used has an impact on the efficiency of file access, storage utilization, and file fragmentation.

5. Directory Structure:

- How files are stored and accessed on a storage device is determined by file allocation mechanisms.
- Contiguous allocation, linked allocation, indexed allocation, and a mix of these approaches are common file allocation strategies.
- The allocation mechanism used has an impact on the efficiency of file access, storage utilization, and file fragmentation.

6. File Access and Permissions:

- File systems control file access rights, guaranteeing data security and privacy.
- Which users or groups may read, write, or execute files is determined by access control lists (ACLs) or permission settings.
- Individual individuals or groups can be granted permissions, giving them fine-grained control over file access.

7. Disk Space Management:

- Disc space management entails monitoring and assigning available storage space on storage devices.

- The file system manages file insertion and removals, as well as keeping track of free and allotted space.
- File compression, file system defragmentation, and quota management are examples of disc space management approaches.

8. File System Integrity and Recovery:

- File systems use techniques to keep data intact and recover from mistakes or system failures.
- Journaling, checksums, and duplicate copies of important file system structures all contribute to data consistency.
- File system consistency checks and recovery processes are done in the case of a system crash or power outage to return the file system to a consistent state.

Storage management and efficient file systems are critical for organizing and safeguarding data on storage devices. They let users to effectively store, retrieve, and manage files and folders. The file system and storage management components of the operating system provide data reliability, accessibility, and optimal storage resource utilization.

5.4 Introduction to System Software and Utilities:

A collection of programmes that aid in the operation and management of a computer system is referred to as system software. It connects application software with computer hardware by delivering vital services and utilities. Here is an overview of system software and its main components:

1. Operating Systems (OS):

- The operating system is the fundamental software that handles computer hardware resources and serves as a user interface.
- It covers responsibilities including process management, memory management, file system management, device management, and user interface.

Windows, macOS, Linux, Android, and iOS are examples of operating systems.

2. Device Drivers:

- Device drivers are software components that allow the operating system to connect with and communicate with hardware devices.
- They serve as an interface via which the operating system may manage and access the functionality of devices like as printers, scanners, network cards, and graphics cards.
- Device drivers guarantee that the operating system and hardware devices work together properly.

3. System Libraries:

- System libraries are sets of precompiled functions and routines that provide programmes with common functionality.
- They contain libraries for activities including input/output operations, mathematical calculations, networking, and GUI creation.
- System libraries make application development easier by offering ready-to-use routines and assuring system compatibility.

4. Utility Programs:

- Utility programmes are software applications that aid in system administration, maintenance, and troubleshooting.

- They carry out a variety of tasks, including disc cleanup, file compression, antivirus scanning, system backup and recovery, and system optimization.
- Utility programmes improve overall system performance, security, and efficiency.

5. Language Translators:

- High-level programming languages are converted into machine-readable code via language translators.
- Compilers turn source code into executable programmes, interpreters run code without compilation, and assemblers translate assembly language into machine code.
- Language translators allow application software to run on computer hardware.

6. Virtualization Software:

- Virtualization software enables the construction and control of virtual machines (VMs) on a single physical computer that run numerous operating systems or software environments.

- Virtualization allows for the effective use of hardware resources, the isolation of software environments, and simplified software deployment and testing.

7. Debuggers and Profilers:

- Debuggers assist software developers in detecting and correcting programming flaws (bugs) in their code.
- Profilers examine programme execution to discover performance bottlenecks, memory leaks, and other areas for optimization.
- Debuggers and profilers help in the creation and optimization of software, increasing programme dependability and performance.

System software and utilities are required for computer systems to work properly and to be managed. They provide as the basis for executing programmes, controlling hardware resources, assuring system performance, and delivering a pleasant user experience. Computers would be unable to execute programmes or utilize their hardware capabilities without system software.

5.5|Software and its types:

A collection of programmes, data, and instructions that inform a computer how to accomplish certain tasks is referred to as software. It is an important component of a computer system that allows users to do various jobs and solve difficulties. Software is divided into two categories: system software and application software.

1. System Software:

- System software is a collection of programmes that maintains and controls computer hardware and serves as a platform for application software to run on.
- The operating system (OS) is the principal system software that organizes and regulates the computer system's general functioning.
- Device drivers, system utilities, programming language translators (compilers, interpreters, assemblers), and virtualization software are examples of system software components.
- System software ensures that hardware resources are used efficiently, offers an interface for user

interaction, and aids in the execution of application software.

2. Application Software:

Programmes created to execute certain tasks or give functionality to users are referred to as application software.

It is designed to fulfil the demands of certain users and can range from simple to complicated applications.

There are several forms of application software, including:

a. Productivity Software: Document, spreadsheet, presentation, and database creation, editing, and management software. Word processors, spreadsheet programmes, presentation software, and database management systems are among examples.

b. Multimedia Software: Software that is used to create, edit, and play multimedia content such as photos, videos, and audio. Photo editing software, video editing software, media players, and graphic design tools are among examples.

c. Communication Software: Email clients, instant messaging programmes, video conferencing tools, and web browsers are examples of software that promotes user communication.

d. Entertainment Software: Video games, interactive media, virtual reality apps, and media streaming platforms are examples of entertainment software.

e. Educational Software: Educational software that includes simulations and interactive learning experiences. E-learning platforms, instructional games, language learning software, and scientific simulations are all part of it.

f. Business Software: Accounting software, inventory management systems, customer relationship management (CRM) software, and enterprise resource planning (ERP) systems are examples of business software.

g. Utilities: Software tools that aid in system administration, maintenance, and troubleshooting. Antivirus applications, disc cleansing programmes, file compression utilities, and backup software are among them.

Application software is created to address unique user needs and to provide capabilities adapted to different areas and businesses. Users engage with application software to complete specified tasks, solve problems, and reach their objectives.

Both system software and application software are essential components of a computer system, enabling effective and productive use of hardware resources while meeting the different demands of users.

Unit 6: Computer Networks

6.1|Basics of Computer Networks and their Significance:

The connecting of many computers and other devices to facilitate communication and data exchange is referred to as a computer network. They are critical in contemporary computing because they enable the sharing of resources, information, and services. Here are the fundamentals of computer networks and their importance:

1. Definition and Components:

- A computer network is a linked collection of equipment such as computers, servers, routers, switches, and wireless access points.
- Local Area Networks (LANs), Wide Area Networks (WANs), and Metropolitan Area Networks (MANs) are the three types of networks depending on their geographical reach.

2. Communication and Data Exchange:

- Computer networks allow devices to connect with one another and share data.

- They make it easier to transfer files, messages, emails, and other types of digital data across linked devices.

3. Resource Sharing:

- Printers, scanners, storage devices, and internet connections may all be shared via networks.
- Users may access shared resources from anywhere on the network, which improves cooperation and efficiency in a shared workplace.

4. Internet Connectivity:

- The internet, a worldwide network of networks, is built on computer networks.
- Users may access a huge array of information, services, and resources available internationally by connecting to the internet.

5. Collaboration and Communication:

- Networks enable individuals and groups to collaborate and communicate with one another.
- They allow for real-time communication by using email, instant messaging, audio and video conferencing, and collaboration platforms.

6. Centralized Data Storage:

- Networks provide centralized data storage on servers, allowing different users to access and exchange data from a single point.
- Centralized storage improves network users' data protection, backup, and accessibility.

7. Scalability and Flexibility:

- Networks can be readily expanded to match the increase in the number of devices and users.
- They provide flexibility by enabling devices to connect and disconnect from the network without interfering with overall network connection.

8. Security and Privacy:

- To safeguard data and resources from unauthorized access and threats, computer networks require security measures.
- Firewalls, encryption, access restrictions, and authentication are examples of network security techniques that secure data confidentiality and integrity.

9. Business Efficiency and Productivity:

- Networks increase organizational efficiency and productivity by facilitating quicker communication, resource sharing, and collaborative processes.
- They improve company operations, make remote work easier, and aid in the integration of multiple systems and applications.

10. Internet of Things (IoT):

- Computer networks serve as the foundation for the Internet of Things, which connects common things to the internet to enable data interchange and automation.
- Smart homes, industrial automation, intelligent transportation systems, and other cutting-edge applications are made possible by IoT networks.

Communication, knowledge exchange, and resource utilization have all been transformed by computer networks. Individuals, corporations, educational institutions, and governments all rely on them to connect, collaborate, and get access to global resources. The importance of computer networks is obvious in today's linked world, pushing technological developments and changing how people live, work, and communicate.

6.2 Network Topologies and Protocols:

Topologies and protocols for computer networks are critical components. They determine the network's physical and logical structure, as well as how devices connect and share data. Here's a quick rundown of network topologies and protocols:

Network Topologies:

1. Bus Topology:

- Devices in a bus topology are linked by a shared communication connection known as a bus.
- Data is sent over the bus, and devices receive and process the data that is meant for them.
- To prevent signal reflection, a terminator is put at either end of the bus.
- Bus topologies are simple and inexpensive, but they might suffer from performance problems if there are too many devices or cable defects.

2. Star Topology:

- Devices in a star topology are linked to a central device, such as a switch or hub.

- All device communication is routed through the central device.
- If one device fails, the remainder of the network is unaffected, making star topologies dependable and simple to operate.
- The central device, on the other hand, can become a single point of failure.

3. Ring Topology:

- Ring topologies link components in a closed loop to form a ring.
- Each gadget is linked to its neighbours, and data flows in only one direction around the ring.
- Devices serve as repeaters, amplifying the signal and transmitting it to the next device.
- Ring topologies give equitable network access and are appropriate for networks with a known number of devices.

4. Mesh Topology:

- Mesh topologies link devices directly to one another, establishing many interconnections.

- Every device in the network has a dedicated link to every other device.
- Mesh topologies provide redundancy and fault tolerance, allowing data to be redirected in the event that one link fails.
- Mesh topologies, on the other hand, need additional cabling and might be difficult to build and administer.

Network Protocols:

1. TCP/IP (Transmission Control Protocol/Internet Protocol):

- TCP/IP is the most frequently used protocol suite for internet and private network communication.
- It enables device-to-device communication that is dependable and connection-oriented.
- TCP maintains data transport reliability by establishing a connection, dividing data into packets, and reassembling them at the destination.
- IP is in charge of addressing and routing data packets across networks.

2. Ethernet:

- Ethernet is a popular local area network (LAN) protocol that specifies how data is delivered over a network.
- It employs a bus or star architecture and operates on the OSI model's physical and data link levels.
- Ethernet establishes a set of standards for data transmission, collision detection, and network access.

3. Wi-Fi (Wireless Fidelity):

- Wi-Fi is a wireless networking technology that connects devices to a network without the use of physical wires.
- It is based on the IEEE 802.11 standards and communicates using radio waves.
- Wi-Fi allows users to connect to the internet and local network resources wirelessly.

4. DNS (Domain Name System):

- DNS is a protocol that converts domain names (for example, www.example.com) to IP addresses.
- It allows users to access websites and services by utilizing simple domain names rather than numeric IP addresses.

5. HTTP (Hypertext Transfer Protocol):

- HTTP is a World Wide Web protocol for transmitting hypertext documents.
- It specifies how web browsers and web servers exchange data.
- HTTP is the protocol that is used to visit websites and send and receive online content.

6. FTP (File Transfer Protocol):

- FTP is a network protocol for exchanging data between computers.
- It offers a collection of standard commands and rules.

6.3|Introductino to the Internet and the World Wide Web:

Although the phrases Internet and World Wide Web (WWW) are commonly used interchangeably, they are not synonymous. Here's a rundown of both:

1. The Internet:

- The Internet is a global network of interconnected computers and devices that use protocols such as TCP/IP to communicate.
- It is a massive network that covers the world and links millions of devices such as computers, servers, routers, and mobile phones.
- The Internet allows for communication, data sharing, and access to a wide range of information and services.

2. The World Wide Web (WWW):

- The World Wide Web, sometimes known as the Web, is a collection of interconnected publications and resources that can be accessed over the Internet.
- It is a network of interconnected hypertext texts identifiable by Uniform Resource Locators (URLs).
- Users may browse between webpages on the Web by clicking on hyperlinks, resulting in a web of interrelated information.

3. Web Browsers:

- Web browsers are software applications that allow users to access and explore the World Wide Web. Examples include Google Chrome, Mozilla Firefox, and Microsoft Edge.
- Browsers interpret and display webpages, handle user interactions, and make web resource retrieval easier.

4. Webpages and Websites:

- A website is a single Web document that is often produced in HTML (Hypertext Markup Language).
- Text, photos, multimedia components, and linkages to other webpages or external resources can all be found on a webpage.
- A website is a collection of connected information or services comprised of several websites organized under a single domain.

5. Hyperlinks and URLs:

- Hyperlinks, often known as links, are clickable items that connect to other webpages or resources.
- They let users to browse between webpages and access various portions of the Internet.
- Hyperlinks are text or graphic representations that, when clicked, take the user to the linked material.

- URLs (Uniform Resource Locators) are Internet addresses that uniquely identify webpages and services.

6. Web Servers:

- Web servers are computers or systems that store and provide users with webpages and other web content.
- When a user requests a webpage, the web server handles the request, obtains the desired material, and returns it to the user's web browser for display.

7. Web Development:

- Web development is the process of creating, designing, and maintaining websites and web applications.
- It entails duties including authoring HTML, CSS, and JavaScript code, developing user interfaces, and maintaining server-side technology.

The World Wide Web's core infrastructure and connections are provided by the Internet. The Web, on the other hand, is an information environment accessed by web browsers that allows users to travel, search, and engage with a huge diversity of websites, webpages, and online resources. It has transformed global communication, information exchange, and access to knowledge.

6.4|Network Security and Data Protection:

Data protection and network security are critical components of computer systems and networks for ensuring data confidentiality, integrity, and availability. An overview of network security and data protection is provided below:

1. Network Security:

- Implementing network security measures protects the network infrastructure, devices, and data from unauthorized access, threats, and vulnerabilities.
- Its goal is to prevent unauthorized access, data breaches, network assaults, and data theft.
- Firewalls, intrusion detection and prevention systems (IDPS), virtual private networks (VPNs), network segmentation, access restrictions, and

encryption are examples of network security mechanisms.

2. Data Encryption:

- Encryption is the process of turning data into an unreadable and secure format to prevent unauthorized access.
- It ensures that even if the data is intercepted, it remains unreadable in the absence of the encryption key.
- Asymmetric encryption (using public and private key pairs) and symmetric encryption (using a shared key) are two types of encryption algorithms.

3. Access Controls:

- Based on their responsibilities, permissions, and authentication, access controls limit and manage user access to network resources.
- Passwords, biometrics, and two-factor authentication are examples of strong authentication systems that improve access security.

- Access controls aid in the prevention of unauthorized users gaining access to sensitive data or important network resources.

4. Firewalls:

- Firewalls serve as a barrier between internal and external networks (such as the internet).
- Based on specified security criteria, they monitor and manage network traffic.
- Firewalls can identify and prevent harmful activity, as well as block unauthorized access attempts and filter incoming and outgoing traffic.

5. Intrusion Detection and Prevention Systems (IDPS):

- IDPS analyze network data for suspicious or malicious activity that might signal an incursion.
- They investigate suspected security vulnerabilities by analyzing network packets, log files, and system activities.
- IDPS may produce warnings, prevent attacks by taking proactive actions, and offer thorough data for analysis and incident response.

6. Virtual Private Networks (VPNs):

- VPNs establish safe, encrypted connections across public networks like the internet.
- They give secure remote access to private networks, allowing users to safely send data.
- VPNs are often used to secure connections for distant employees and branch offices, as well as to protect sensitive data during transmission.

7. Data Backup and Disaster Recovery:

- Backup and disaster recovery procedures are critical for assuring data availability and security.
- Backing up data on a regular basis helps to prevent data loss in the case of hardware problems, natural catastrophes, or cyberattacks.
- Backup copies of data should be securely kept elsewhere to ensure its availability in the event of a disaster.

8. Security Awareness and Education:

- Network security entails not only technological precautions, but also user awareness and education.
- Regular training programmes may assist users in understanding recommended practices for security, identifying phishing efforts, and adhering to safe data management processes.

9. Compliance and Regulatory Requirements:

- Organizations may be subject to industry-specific data protection rules and compliance obligations.
- GDPR (General Data Protection Regulation) and HIPAA (Health Insurance Portability and Accountability Act) compliance frameworks set criteria and principles for data protection and privacy.

Network security and data protection are ongoing processes that need constant monitoring, upgrades, and modifications to handle new threats and vulnerabilities. Organizations may limit risks and safeguard their networks, data, and sensitive information from unauthorized access, breaches, and cyberattacks by deploying rigorous security measures.

Unit 7: Troubleshooting and Maintenance

7.1|Computer Problems and Troubleshooting Techniques:

Computer difficulties can arise for a variety of causes, ranging from hardware malfunctions to software flaws. Here are some examples of frequent computer problems and their solutions:

1. Slow Performance:

- Close any unwanted programmes or processes that are operating in the background.
- Remove temporary files and clear up disc space by doing a disc cleanup.
- If hardware components, such as RAM or storage, are insufficient for the system's needs, upgrade them.
- Perform a malware scan to look for any harmful software that may be interfering with performance.

2. System Freezing or Crashing:

- Overheating may be avoided by providing appropriate airflow and maintaining the computer's cooling system.
- Upgrade device drivers to the most recent versions.
- Examine your computer for malware and viruses.
- To discover any damaged RAM modules, do a system memory test.
- Check for software conflicts or concerns with compatibility.

3. Internet Connectivity Issues:

- Restart both the router and the modem.
- Examine the physical connections and cords.
- The network drivers should be updated.
- Reset the network configuration.
- Check with your Internet Service Provider (ISP) for any service interruptions or configuration problems.

4. Blue Screen of Death (BSOD):

- Restart the computer and look for any recent hardware or software modifications that could have contributed to the problem.
- Drivers for devices should be updated.

- Scan the system for malware and viruses.
- To return to a prior stable configuration, use system restore.
- Seek expert help if the condition persists.

5. Hardware Failure:

- Examine the physical connections and cords.
- Ascertain that all components are correctly positioned.
- Test the hardware on a different computer to see whether it is the source of the problem.
- The defective hardware component should be replaced or repaired.

6. Software Errors of Application Crashes:

- Upgrade the programme to the most recent version.
- Restart the computer and open the programme again.
- If the problem persists, reinstall the programme.
- Check for any incompatible software or settings.

7. Unresponsive Peripherals:

- Examine the peripheral devices' physical connections.
- Check to see if the device drivers are up to date.

- Reboot your computer and reconnect the device.
- Test the peripheral on another computer to see whether the problem is hardware or software.
- If required, replace the peripheral.

8. Data Loss:

- Stop utilizing the afflicted storage device if possible to avoid further data overwriting.
- To recover deleted files, use data recovery software or services.
- Backup essential files on a regular basis to avoid data loss in the future.

In general, diagnosing computer issues entails a methodical approach that includes recognizing symptoms, inspecting hardware and software components, and implementing viable remedies. If the problem persists or is above your level of experience, it is best to seek professional help.

7.2|System Maintenance and Updates:

System maintenance and upgrades are required to keep your computer functioning efficiently, safely, and securely. The following are some critical components of system maintenance and updates:

1. Operating System Updates:

- Check for and install operating system updates given by the software manufacturer on a regular basis (for example, Windows updates, mac-OS updates, and Linux updates).
- Bug fixes, security patches, and performance enhancements are frequently included in operating system upgrades.
- Configure your machine to download and install updates automatically to guarantee you get the most recent fixes.

2. Software Updates:

- Keep all of your installed software up to date, including programmes and drivers.
- Most software programmes have built-in update systems or give automated update alerts.

- Check for and install updates on a regular basis to take advantage of new features, bug fixes, and security upgrades.

3. Antivirus and Security Updates:

- Install trustworthy antivirus software and maintain it up to date with the most recent virus definitions.
- Update your security software on a regular basis to guarantee that it can identify and guard against new threats.
- Enable automatic updates for your security software to keep safe from new threats.

4. Disk Cleanup and Optimization:

- Perform disc cleanup on a regular basis to eliminate temporary files, unneeded programmes, and redundant system files.
- To optimize file placement and enhance system speed, use disc optimization programmes (such as Disc Defragmenter on Windows).

5. Data Backup:

- Create a regular data backup schedule to safeguard your crucial files and papers.

- Backups can be created using external hard drives, online storage services, or backup software.
- Test your backups on a regular basis to verify they are working and recoverable.

6. Hardware Maintenance:

- Keep your computer physically clean by dusting off the components on a regular basis and providing appropriate airflow.
- To avoid overheating, inspect and clean the cooling system.
- If required, inspect and reseat hardware components like as RAM modules and expansion cards.
- As needed, replace defective hardware components.

7. Passwords and Security:

- Update and tighten your passwords for your computer, internet accounts, and applications on a regular basis.
- For secure password management, use complicated passwords or consider using a password manager.
- To add an extra degree of protection, enable two-factor authentication wherever possible.

8. Regular System Scans:

- Regularly scan your machine with antivirus software to look for malware, viruses, and other security concerns.
- To provide ongoing protection, schedule automated scans to run in the background.

System maintenance and upgrades are continual activities that benefit your computer's performance, security, and reliability. You can guarantee a reliable and safe computer environment by doing these actions on a regular basis.

7.3|Data Backup and Recovery:

Data backup and recovery are essential for safeguarding your critical information and assuring their availability in the case of data loss or system failure. Here's a quick rundown of data backup and recovery:

1. Data Backup:

- The act of making copies of your files and storing them in a different location or device is known as data backup.
- It allows you to recover your data if your original files are lost, damaged, or unavailable.
- Among the several backup solutions are:
- Full back up: A full copy of all files and folders is created.
- Only back up the changes that have occurred since the last backup.
- Differential backup is the process of backing up changes made since the last complete backup.
- Backups are stored on remote servers using cloud services.
- Backups stored on external hard drives, network-attached storage (NAS), or other local storage devices are referred to as local backups.

2. Backup Strategies:

- Implement a backup system that meets your requirements while also ensuring data redundancy.
- Consider combining local and offshore backups for enhanced security.

- Schedule backups on a regular basis to guarantee that the most recent versions of your data are saved.

3. Data Recovery:

- The process of recovering lost, destroyed, or damaged files from backups is known as data recovery.
- In the event of data loss, take the following steps:
- Determine the reason of the data loss, whether it was due to an accident, hardware failure, or software flaws.
- Determine the backup location for your data.
- Restore the missing files from your backup to their original or a different place.
- Check the restored data's integrity and accessibility.

4. Test and Verify Backups:

- Test your backup system on a regular basis to guarantee its dependability and efficacy.
- Perform test restorations of a sample set of files on a regular basis to ensure backup integrity.
- Check to ensure that your backup system is gathering all required files and data.

5. Automated Backup Tools:

- To simplify the backup process and assure consistency, use automatic backup solutions or software.
- These programmes may schedule backups, make incremental backups, and offer data compression and encryption options.

6. Cloud Backup Services:

- Consider utilizing trusted suppliers' cloud backup services.
- Cloud backup provides safe storage, automated backups, and access from any location with an internet connection.

7. Versioning and File History:

- If versioning or file history features are available, enable them.
- These tools save numerous copies of your work, allowing you to go back in time if necessary.

Remember that data backup is a proactive approach to prevent data loss, thus it's critical to establish a backup plan that meets your demands and to make backups on a regular basis. In the unfortunate case of data loss, having a dependable backup solution in place can assist you in recovering your vital information while minimizing downtime.

7.4|Best Practices for Computer Security and Privacy:

It is critical to preserve your personal information, sensitive data, and prevent unauthorized access by ensuring computer security and privacy. The following are some best practices to follow:

1. Use Strong and Unique Passwords:
   - Make strong and complicated passwords with a mix of capital and lowercase letters, numbers, and special characters.
   - For each online account or service, use a different password.
   - Consider using a password manager to store and create passwords securely.

2. Enable Two-Factor Authentication (2FA):

- Enable two-factor authentication wherever feasible to provide an extra degree of security.
- In addition to your password, 2FA needs a second form of authentication, such as a verification number texted to your mobile device.

3. Keep Software Up to Date:

- Update your operating system, programmes, and software on a regular basis to guarantee you have the most recent security updates and bug fixes.
- When feasible, enable automatic updates.

4. Use Antivirus and Security Software:

- To guard against malware, viruses, and other dangerous threats, install trusted antivirus and security software.
- Keep your antivirus software up to date with the most recent virus definitions.

5. Be Cautious of Phishing Attempts:

- Be wary of any questionable emails, texts, or phone calls requesting personal or financial information.
- Clicking on dodgy websites or downloading files from unknown sources should be avoided.

- Before sharing sensitive information, confirm the veracity of requests or interactions.

6. Secure Your Wireless Network:

- To prevent unauthorized access, create a strong password for your Wi-Fi network.
- For safe wireless connection, use encryption methods like WPA2 or WPA3.

7. Regularly Backup Your Data:

- Backup your vital files and data on a regular basis to an external hard drive, cloud storage, or other safe backup alternatives.
- Test your backups on a regular basis to verify they are working and can be restored if necessary.

8. Practice Safe Browsing Habits:

- When accessing new websites, use caution and avoid downloading anything from untrustworthy sources.
- When submitting sensitive information, such as during online transactions, use secure and encrypted websites (look for "https" in the URL).

9. Be Mindful of Social Media Privacy:

- Examine and update your social media privacy settings to manage what information is exposed to others.
- Be cautious while disclosing personal information in public.

10. Secure Physical Access:

- Use locks, passwords, or biometric authentication to keep your computer and other devices physically safe.
- Keep an eye on who has access to your gadgets, especially in public.

11. Educate Yourself and Stay Informed:

- Keep up to current on the most recent security risks, trends, and best practices.
- To build excellent habits, educate yourself and your family members on computer security and privacy.

Remember that computer security is an ongoing process, and it's critical to remain proactive and diligent in safeguarding your data and privacy. You may dramatically improve your computer security and protect your personal information by applying these recommended practices.

Conclusion:-

We addressed the essential principles of computer systems in "Computer Systems: A Comprehensive Guide to the Basics," providing you with a solid foundation of knowledge. This book will be an important resource whether you are seeking a career in technology or simply want to comprehend the technology that surrounds you. Understanding the fundamentals of computer systems allows you to unleash unlimited possibilities and confidently traverse the ever-changing digital universe. So, go ahead and enter into the intriguing world of computer systems!

www.ingramcontent.com/pod-product-compliance
Lightning Source LLC
Chambersburg PA
CBHW070423220526
45466CB00004B/1514